THE
COUNTERFEIT
CHRISTIAN

THE COUNTERFEIT CHRISTIAN

A Woman's Journey From
Darkness to Redemption

ROBIN BYERS

XULON PRESS

Xulon Press
2301 Lucien Way #415
Maitland, FL 32751
407.339.4217
www.xulonpress.com

Unless otherwise indicated, Scripture quotations taken from the Holy Bible, New Living Translation (NLT). Copyright ©1996, 2004, 2007 by Tyndale House Foundation. Used by permission of Tyndale House Publishers, Inc.

Scripture quotations taken from the Holy Bible, New International Version (NIV). Copyright © 1973, 1978, 1984, 2011 by Biblica, Inc.™. Used by permission. All rights reserved.

Scripture quotations taken from the New King James Version (NKJV). Copyright © 1982 by Thomas Nelson, Inc. Used by permission. All rights reserved.

The cover art for this book was done by my talented friend Jeanette Inman. It is one of many paintings and other forms of art she created during her lifetime. Sadly, her family and friends lost her to cancer on November 11, 2017. As amazing as her art is to me, the most remarkable thing about her was her strong Christian witness. In the brief time I came to know her as my friend (only about two years), she brought me into the presence of God every time we had a visit. Her testimony and the grace with which she lived her eight years' journey with cancer never ceased to amaze me. Her legacy is her Christian love and witness, her children, and her incredible art.

*Art available on http//jvonne_inman.artistswebsites.com (Fine Art America)

Paperback ISBN-13: 978-1-66281-929-2
Ebook ISBN-13: 978-1-66281-930-8

Dedication:

This writing is dedicated to God and my parents, who got me through my worst times with their love and support. They were such a blessing to me in my darkest days. I am especially grateful for God, who never deserted me despite my dark state of mind. No doubt my survival is due to the love of God and my parents.

TABLE OF CONTENTS

*Note: This scripture really speaks to me, particularly because of my life experiences.

Psalm 139:1-6, 13-16 NIV

O Lord, you have searched me, and you know me. You know when I sit and when I rise; you perceive my thoughts from afar. You discern my going out and my lying down; you are familiar with all my ways. Before a word is on my tongue you know it completely, O Lord. You hem me in behind and before; you have laid your hand on me. Such knowledge is too wonderful for me, too lofty for me to attain.

For you created my inmost being, you knit me together in my mother's womb. I praise you because I am fearfully and wonderfully made; your works are wonderful. I know that full well. My frame was not hidden from you when I was made in the secret place. When I was woven together in the depths of the earth, your eyes saw my unformed body. All the days ordained for me were written in your book before one of them came to be.

Note: Some of the names have been changed to protect the identity of certain characters.

Acknowledgements:

To the boyfriend of my youth, whose story was an important part of mine; please know it was never my intention to hurt you. Our relationship was mainly good rather than bad, and my memories of that time are mostly fond ones. My purpose for writing this book is to help young couples dealing with unplanned pregnancy as we did. My prayer is that this narrative will influence others to choose more life-affirming options, as well as to illustrate there is more that meets the eye in experiencing the "right to choose."

My thanks are extended to the following people.:

My family, in appreciation for all that my parents did for me. They showed they loved me and did not give up on me, even when things seemed hopeless. For my brother Mark and sister Jodi who were my first friends, my husband John who I thank God for every day, and our beautiful children. Renee, Eric, and my stepdaughter Chelsea.. Meeting my husband and raising our children was a major turning point in my life. It has been both an adventure and a blessing to see our children grow and mature into the people that they are.

My friend Judy for believing me capable of writing and pursuing publication of this book, as well as influencing my faith walk.

My friend Penny for being a supportive Christian friend, and for having gone to the Creation Festival with me.

My friend Anita, who proofread my messy hand-written transcript and did the first edit, as well as helped get my story into proper form for submission. Many thanks!

Introduction

This story was written to illustrate there is always hope, no matter how dark circumstances may be. I make no excuses for my past; it was not pretty. My prayer is for this story to encourage women who have gone through having an abortion to see there is hope and a future beyond the experience of abortion.

To women considering abortion, please stop and consider other alternatives. This is your chance to choose life over death for your unborn child! There are many agencies who assist with pregnancy, childbirth, and adoption. In addition, there are some that help with medical care and counseling.

When I first became pregnant at the age of twenty-one, abortion seemed to be the easy way out. In fact, the procedure itself was not even close to being the worst part of the whole thing. Much later, I better understood abortion stops a beating heart. Had I allowed myself to think of "it" as a baby, the abortion never would have happened. For decades afterwards, I continued to beat myself up with remembered guilt and "what ifs." Anytime the topic of abortion came up in the news or something I read, it was like salt in my emotional wound. It has taken me thirty-three years to allow Jesus to take my burden from me. At the age of fifty-four, I have finally made peace with myself and my past. God has healed my emotional scars, and Jesus has broken the chains of pain that held me for so long! I praise God every day for my life, my husband, and our children. My prayer is that this story will bless and encourage you.

*Note- I wrote the following poem in June 2004. At the time, it was the only way to express how I felt.

Hopefully, it will help give insight into the long-term psychological effects connected with abortion. This is not to say that my experience was typical but rather perhaps a more extreme scenario. In my reading on this subject, however, women often experience depression as well as suicidal thoughts post-abortion. These emotional and spiritual scars often haunt them long after their bodies have physically healed.

A Mother's Heart

Where are the children of my youth? I let them go…
didn't know the pain would come to be my constant companion,
nor did I know how many, many, times I'd be reminded of my past,
and my decisions that altered my destiny,
caused such anguish and grief,
nothing could fill the void…
a gaping, empty hole inside,
I WAS SO ASHAMED,
Till children came into my life,
Helped take away the pain,
Made me feel whole again,
Easing my shame, if not the past,
And I could feel forgiven by God, and myself at last!

- In all honesty, it was ten years after this poem was written that I felt forgiven and free, after professing to be a Christian for twenty-four years.

Chapter One

FAMILY LIFE

I have always felt like depression ran in my family, at least on my mother's side. Mom suffered from depression for the first ten years of my life. She seemed okay to me, most of the time. On a purely sub-conscious level, perhaps I had some awareness of her struggle. I know she probably tried to hide it from us as her children. Like most moms in the sixties, my mom was a housewife who did not work outside our home, at least not until we were all school age.

Our church family photo

My dad worked a lot of hours, sometimes working a second job to support the family. He worked as a line-man for the phone company, and he often had to work overtime on what he called "trouble." Dad frequently seemed to be in a bad mood when he came home from work. As children, we learned to tread lightly so we would not make his mood worse. My view was that his long, hard days at work made him that way.

He would get mad at the three of us for laughing or just talking at the dinner table. Perhaps he subscribed to the philosophy;

"Children should be seen and not heard." In any case, it seemed that he wanted dinner time quiet.

Mom mostly kept status quo at home because it was pointless to get into an argument with Dad about anything. He was always right, no matter what. Although she did not agree with how Dad handled the finances, she mostly kept quiet about that too. One of my mom's friends suggested she might be happier if she made her own money. This turned out to be good advice. My mom liked working as a waitress and quickly made friends with her co-workers. The bonus was that her job took the pressure off Dad to be the only breadwinner. Mom remained in that job until the business got sold. She retired not long after that happened.

Dad was extremely strict with Jodi, Mark, and me. I believe this was partially because of the way he was raised. He had grown up being responsible for helping his sister cook and clean at a young age because his mother had to support the family by teaching piano lessons. His dad had never held a job long, due to him quitting in anger or getting fired. As a result, our dad seemed to have less security in his living situation than our household had.

Growing up that way, no doubt, shaped the person he became. It seemed his main role in life was to command respect from his children, even if that meant he was an intimidating presence in our lives. He loved us, yes, but was incapable of showing it in a tangible way.

Unfortunately, Dad lived inside walls of his own making for much of his life. I have always felt his distance from us was due to unresolved issues from his past. These same issues fed the anger that was often just below the surface of his emotions. He took the responsibility of raising his family seriously and demonstrated that with his strong work ethic.

Growing up, I often felt that Dad did not love or approve of me, perhaps because he did not show affection toward me or my siblings, for that matter. This was far from the truth as later in life, he showed he loved me because he did not give up on me. Dad showed he loved us in his own way in how he worked so hard to support us.

Dad was very friendly and outgoing with his friends and other adults. This was quite opposite of what we typically saw at home. He was usually the task master or disciplinarian. However, when we went on vacation, he was a different person. He smiled more, laughed more, and seemed to enjoy being together with his family. It was at these times we felt closest to him and that he did indeed love us, unlike at home where the atmosphere was often tense and everyone walked on eggshells to keep the peace.

Though when Dad would take us camping or canoeing as a family or sometimes played his guitar for us, it felt like it was a way too that he showed he cared. These activities could not replace the affection we needed from our parents, but they did help bond us as a family. Much later when we had our own children, that changed. It seemed like being grandparents made them both more affectionate toward the three of us.

Mom was always counterpoint to Dad in the way she dealt with us. She was much kinder and gentler. She was far easier to talk to. She saw me as the loner and book reader. My sister was seen as the outgoing and funny one. She was the peacemaker. My brother was a combination of rebel and victim of Dad's illogical disciplinarian side.

Mom made us feel loved and secure. She took an interest in our school-work and artwork. She was the one who made sure we went to church. She has been my confidante, ally, and most trusted advisor. Mom was then and still is my first and forever best friend. My brother and sister saw our child-hood from a slightly different perspective than I did. Jodi felt like Dad was unfair to Mark, often making him a "gofer," when Dad did home projects. She said it seemed like Dad got jealous when Mark got to play, so he kept him busy. Jodi recalled that her and Mark often got into trouble together, resulting in heavy-handed discipline. Surprisingly, Jodi characterized the discipline we received as consistent. However, she did not go so far as to say that it was fair.

Chapter Two

The World We Grew Up In

Despite having a heavily disciplined childhood, all three of us had the consensus that it was mostly a happy one. Our childhood was lived over the tumultuous decades of the sixties and seventies. Our world was rapidly changing and was racing toward the future. Social norms had shifted with the times. The women's liberation movement put women into the work force in far greater numbers than in previous generations. Birth control pills came out in 1960, and Roe vs. Wade* was passed into law in 1973. These events made it possible for the sexual revolution to start. It also influenced how most people perceived morality. Suddenly people living together without being married increased exponentially. Divorce was made easier. Couples getting divorced increased as well. Another consequence of both no-fault divorce** and women working outside the home was "latchkey kids." Latchkey kids were defined as children who were home without supervision for some part of the day. This typically occurred before or after the school day until a parent returned home from work. Family units trended away from the "Nuclear Family" or all family members living together with both parents.

Even amid all these social changes, it was still an age of innocence. Cable television had yet to be invented. There were just a handful of channels without the benefit of the remote. Realistic video games, cell phones, and personal computers were still in the realm of science fiction. It is hard now to imagine no internet, no social media, and no personal computers that provide endless amounts of information around the clock. As difficult as our childhood sometimes was, I am truly thankful for the simplicity of our lives back then. Being the eldest of the three, it was often difficult for me to be the trailblazer as I tended to be very reserved and introspective.

*Footnote- Roe vs. Wade was legislation passed in 1973 that legalized abortion.

**No-fault divorce- a mutual split (mutual consent) where neither party takes the blame for breakup of marriage. The then-Governor of California Ronald Reagan signed the nation's first no-fault divorce bill in 1969. Most other states followed suit in the decade and a half that followed.

Chapter Three

School Days
and Bullies

When I first entered school, it seemed that I was one of the smallest, skinniest kids in my class. My painful shyness and sensitivity, coupled with my size, made me an easy target for bullying. It was mostly mean boys making fun of my name on the bus. Later, a girl much taller and stronger than me threatened to beat me up. It was rare for me to even talk, so it was not because of something I had said. There were also the girls who excluded me from their group of friends and would not pick me for teams in gym class. In sixth grade, there was a trio of girls who bullied me. The ringleader would tell me to make a certain face, and I would comply in hopes of gaining acceptance. Then the same girl would say, "Isn't she cute?" Then all three would laugh. I was utterly humiliated. Unfortunately, this is common behavior for girls who are in the so-called popular crowd. When I complained to my mom about the bullies, she told me not to let them see me cry. Normally, I did not cry easily anyway. However, I took her advice quite literally and stopped crying altogether. Mom started calling me "hard-hearted Hannah" because even sad movies did not make me cry. I did not take any offense to this but just took it as fact.

Despite my shyness, I had a small circle of friends. They were all quiet, somewhat shy girls like myself. It was my fellow bookworms who helped make my days at school more bearable. Mom and Dad had decided to hold me back in sixth grade due to my abysmal grades. No doubt I probably had some undiagnosed learning disability like ADD. Another issue was my inability to get homework in on time. In fact, I was once spanked in front of my fifth-grade class by the teacher for that reason.

One of the reasons I rarely spoke at school was for fear of looking stupid. This was to be avoided at all costs. In any case, my bullies were moving on to middle school, giving me a chance at a new beginning.

The prospect of getting to know an entire new group of kids was terrifying to me, but in the end, the second sixth grade year was not nearly as bad as the year before. It came as a big blow to me when my close friend Joyce had to move a long distance away. We tried to maintain our friendship via letters, cards, and visits. Unfortunately, we lost touch much later when she married.

Once I made the transition to middle school, I met my new best friend, Carrie. She was not like anyone I had met before. Carrie had a certain confidence that I lacked. She did not seem to care what other people thought of her. We stayed friends all through middle school, but shortly before high school, her dad got a job transfer to Nevada. We wrote to each other, but eventually that tapered off and quit altogether. Both of our lives were busy and changing, so it was not surprising that we were not able to stay in touch.

The first two years of high school were not much different from elementary and middle school. My parents had gotten braces for my teeth, which gave me a new reason to be self-conscious. They were to remain on until the end of my junior year. Initially I fought getting the braces, but my grandmother convinced me to get them. She told me they would give me straight teeth and a nice smile. I am glad I took her advice on that. Now aside from the braces, I was still extremely shy and skinny. I was convinced I was ugly as well. My nose seemed too big for my face, and my hair was too thick and was a drab shade of brown. The only thing I liked about myself was my hazel eyes. Everything else was boring and ordinary.

My body seemed to be stuck at middle-school proportions. In other words, there was no need for me to wear a bra. Not unlike the boys in middle school, the ones at the bus stop were merciless in the taunting that they directed at my sister and me, using words such as surfboards, sunken treasure chests, and carpenter's dreams. It did not matter to me that it was their immaturity that made them behave this way. Their teasing still stung. My only comeback was, "I would rather be flat than fat." The poem "Love's Story" – (was written in 1978 about my secret crushes.)

Love's Story

Love much too strong to be denied,
The emotion most pure and most beautiful,
Cannot be broken until it is tried,
Love that grows, takes seed and is fruitful,

Love very tender and very dear, shares intimate thoughts and dreams,
It outlasts the test of time and year,
Yet it can be very painful it seems,
When one loves, but is not loved in return, and has to love only in dreams.

Chapter Four

Overcoming Shyness

Years of bullying have a way of eating away at your self-esteem until there is barely any left. Having been bullied for most of my school years, I had no idea how to take a compliment. If anyone ever gave me one, I would turn it into an insult with a self-deprecating remark. Throughout middle school and high school, I had many crushes on boys, although they had no clue about that. One year, a new boy had started to attend our school. Kyle was my biggest crush yet, and he usually walked with his best friend. Whenever they both walked past me in the hall, his friend Jim would make dog noises and laugh. This caused me to blush with embarrassment as white-hot anger seethed inside me. Even in high school, my shyness prevented me from sticking up for myself. Ironically, many years later I discovered that Jim had had a crush on me. It was such a strange turn of events.

At school, my shyness had become a curse, a prison from which I had to break free. My sophomore year was when I finally took action to overcome the shyness that isolated me. My first attempt to "get out of my shell" involved clerking at the school store to force myself to interact with others. Later, I became a reporter for the school newspaper and joined some clubs to further shed some of my shyness. Up until that time, it felt like I was on the outside looking in at everyone else living their lives with me always as the bystander. My life felt boring and tasteless and at the age of sixteen, no fun at all. My reporter position completely terrified me, mainly because it meant interviewing people for articles. My first assignment was to interview my math teacher, who had gotten engaged. He seemed sympathetic to my nervousness and made the interview as easy as possible. Eventually, through more interviews, it became a bit easier. Although these things helped me to overcome my shyness somewhat, there was still the issue of my battered self-esteem.

Chapter Five

EARLY CHURCH
EXPERIENCE

My attendance at church did not help much either. Though our family had always attended church regularly.

Our only excuse for not going to church was if we were sick or on vacation. Church was just tradition for me, an empty ritual that did not touch my heart or mind. My perspective on Christianity was very skewed due to my limited, immature beliefs. One such belief was that if a person attended church regularly, he or she was automatically a Christian. The thing I did not understand about faith at that time was that even if you "borrowed" the faith of your parents, at some point, it must come from within yourself. I took God and faith for granted. I now know that becoming a believer means your whole life is a journey of faith aimed at spending eternity with our Lord and Savior Jesus Christ.

In my latter teen years, the time spent at church grew less and less until in my twenties it was rare for me to darken the door of a church. Despite these lapses, prayer was still part of my life. I mostly recited the Lord's Prayer*, which I had memorized at a younger age. When insomnia became a problem in my early twenties, repetition of that prayer helped me to go to sleep. There were times when doubts assailed my mind regarding the truth of God's existence and His love for me. Even as these questions loomed large for me, my belief was like a candle. It may have flickered in the winds of my anxious thoughts, but it never went completely out.

*The Lord's Prayer -Matthew 6: 9-13 (NKJV)

Our Father in Heaven,

Hallowed be your name,

Your kingdom come, Your will be done,

On earth, as it is in Heaven,

Give us this day our daily bread,

And forgive us our debts as we forgive our debtors,

And do not lead us into temptation,

But deliver us from the evil one

For Yours is the kingdom, and the power, and the glory forever. Amen.

Chapter Six

Experimentation

In my latter wilder teen years of high school, there was experimentation with drugs and alcohol. Mostly, there was alcohol use as an attempt to conquer my debilitating shyness and gain acceptance from my peer group. At the end of my junior year, my braces finally came off, which was a boost to my self-confidence. While hanging out at the roller-skating rink, there was a very brief dating experience I had, which was a very superficial relationship. In the end, it did nothing to help my self-esteem. It was still inconceivable to me that anyone would find me attractive, mainly due to my history with being bullied and the difficult relationship I had with my father. Ironically, out of the three of us siblings, I have the most personality traits in common with our dad. Please do not misunderstand me—although we butted heads more than we got along, he was* still my dad, and I loved him. For me, though, it was not always easy to love him, probably because we were too much alike and perhaps identified traits in each other that we did not care for in ourselves. In any case, even given all of this, I still tended to be attracted to men who resembled my dad to a certain degree. Though my dating life was up to that time non-existent, there were still many silly, hopeless crushes on boys who never even knew I liked them.

*My dad passed away on February 16, 2012, due to complications from his stroke. He was seventy-two years old.

Chapter Seven

First Boyfriend

In the summer of my junior year, it seemed that God or fate stepped into my life. Our family had been invited to a pool party by friends of my parents. I was feeling more self-confident than usual for a change. My braces were off, and my mom had gotten me the bikini I had begged for. She thought it was too old for me because it was black. In my mind, it paired well with my straw hat that had red flowers. When we arrived at the party, many guests were already enjoying the pool. As we entered the pool area, an attractive guy close to my age came up to me and introduced himself. His name was Calvin, and he told me he worked for the hosts of the party. What really shocked me was how easy it was to talk to him. Usually, I had trouble even getting a word out of my mouth around guys. Calvin suggested we get a drink, and we proceeded to get to know each other better poolside. It turned out he was just a few years older than me, and it was exciting to have someone interested in me for a change. When we went into the pool together, however, he kept dunking me to the point that I was getting mad. He later told me it had been an excuse to be near me.

Toward the end of the evening, my family was getting ready to go home. Calvin approached and then asked for my phone number and a date for the following weekend. I accepted, of course, and we made plans for our date later over the phone. It was so thrilling for me to finally be going on a real date with someone who wanted to be with me! That next Saturday, we went out to eat and saw a movie. We talked a lot during the meal and discovered we had much in common. We enjoyed spending time together so much, that we decided to go out again the next weekend.

Shortly after that, we began seeing each other every weekend. Calvin was traveling to my house every time and had asked if we could take turns going to each other's houses every other weekend. The problem was that he lived a good distance from me. My dad had put a limit on how much time I could spend on the phone with him because technically it was long distance, even though he lived only about an hour away from my house. This just made me want to see him more. After we had dated for a month, my parents agreed to let me go to his house, where he lived with his mom and sister. It was close to my birthday, so I had begged and pleaded until I got them to agree, using the excuse that his mom and sister would be there. Calvin was my first boyfriend, and I wanted to see him as much as possible. I wrote "Sitting Alone" for him in 1978.

Sitting Alone

Missing you and wishing you were here, by my side,
No one knows, but the cold wind blows secretly inside me,
It seems surprised to find it has time to be here with my loneliness
I feel the emptiness in my soul as the wind sweeps through my body,
For I have no substance, but the gentle flowing of my being with the wind,
Then my heart hears a sound, so quiet it can barely be heard, the sound made by the falling snow,
It is you, my love, who has come to warm the depths of my frozen soul, with a gentle word or touch.

Chapter Eight

PREGNANCY & ABORTION

I t was after we had dated for a little over a month that Calvin and I made love for the first time. Although I was extremely nervous, it felt like the right thing to do because of our feelings for each other. As for me, it was painful, and I cried afterwards. This prompted Calvin to ask me what was wrong, and the fact I had been a virgin came to light. It was just too embarrassing to tell him beforehand. He told me he felt honored to be my first, which made things feel even more awkward for me because inside my head, all my thoughts screamed that what we had done was wrong. I told him I was not sure if we should ever do it again. We did talk about this and decided to slow things down to accommodate these feelings. Eventually, the physical part of our relationship did resume, because of how we felt about each other. Calvin seemed to love me, and often complimented my appearance, this helped me to feel better about myself.

When we first started to date, it felt weird when he put his arm around me or gave me hugs. I was not used to affection from anyone but my grandparents. After we had been dating for two years, I started to become restless because in high school, I had only gone out with one other boy and had nothing to compare this relationship with. It felt like I needed to date more before making a commitment to him. Our first break-up was hard, but it did not last for an extended period. I missed him too much, and we both wanted to continue in the relationship. Not long after we got back together, I became pregnant due to inconsistent use of the birth control pill. My twenty-first birthday was coming soon, and Calvin wanted to marry me. He had even gotten me a ring. Suddenly, everything seemed to be happening extremely fast. We had been dating close to three years by this time, but I was not ready to decide about the rest of my life. All I could feel was panic and a sense of being trapped. Many thoughts flooded through my mind, as well as images of the whole pregnancy and birth process. The more my mind focused on these things, the more the prospect scared me to death! Because I was feeling so panic-stricken, it became clear to me that I was not ready for marriage or the responsibility of raising a child. Although my religious beliefs told me abortion was wrong, fear overrode everything else in my mind. Calvin begged me to have the baby, even if he had to raise it himself. Unfortunately, my thoughts were centered more on myself and the mess I was in. We talked about having or not having the baby, but we did not agree. Ultimately, I convinced Calvin to go along with the abortion.

This piece of news was hard to break to my mom. She was upset, of course, but she left the decision up to me. What really scared me was the thought of telling my dad. It was difficult for me to imagine how he might react. In the end, he found out after the fact. Honestly, I have no recollection of how we told him or how he reacted. When Calvin and I drove to the clinic, my stomach was in knots. My feelings for the most part swung between guilt and shame. What we planned to do was wrong in the eyes of God. Fear overwhelmed me and motivated all my actions. It was that same fear that colored all my thoughts and blinded me from facing the facts. To tell you the truth, I bought the lie that pro-abortionists put out there. That it is a women's right to do what she wants with her own body is one such lie. They neglect to address the fact that the baby is not part of the women's body. It is part in the sense it grows there but is still a separate being. The staff at the clinic counseled us briefly about other alternatives* but failed to change my mind.

No opportunity to have a sonogram was offered. Perhaps if they had, I would have made a different decision. I would like to think so, anyway, but sadly, we did go through with the planned abortion. My only thought was to get it over with, get past it, and move on with my life. In real life, moving on was not that simple. Calvin was being very caring and supportive the whole time. I really do not know how he did it; my attitude toward him was not good to say the least. Instead of taking any ownership of the situation myself, I blamed and resented him. I placed all the blame on Calvin, even though that was not fair of me.

Afterwards, there was pain, bleeding, and a hollow feeling in my heart. Calvin stayed by my side, even when my mood became bitter and depressed. He tried to cheer me up by taking me to the movies and even a concert that featured my favorite bands. God bless him, he really tried to help me! While in the depressed state, it made me feel even worse that I could not feel better for him. Despite his efforts, depression had taken a hold of me. Nothing could ease the loneliness and emptiness I felt inside.

*Adoptions from the Heart, 5630 Linglestown Road #3012, Harrisburg PA 17112 (expenses paid-open or closed adoption) 717-399-7766

PA Adoption Agencies of America, Heart Gallery, Suite 402, Lancaster, PA 717-642-7200 (adoption agency with wide array of services)

National Resources: Alternative Federal Credit Union (607)273-4611 Toll free 1-877-273-AFCU

(Financial support and education of underserved people.)

Real Alternatives 1-888-Life Aid

(life-affirming free pregnancy and parenting support services)

RealAlternatives.org

Chapter Nine

DEPRESSION, PREGNANCY #2-BREAK UP

My biggest fear was that God had abandoned me and no longer cared for or loved me. Our relationship suffered from what we had been through. Unfortunately, there were more trials on the horizon. At some point, there must have been an evaluation of my mental state. It was determined by a doctor that my diagnosis was Bi-polar disorder and my symptoms required medication. Bi-polar Disorder is characterized by manic mood "highs" and depressive "lows". This illness is a chemical imbalance of the brain, which is also known as a mood disorder.

It is interesting to note that people who suffer from this illness are often creative people, such as artists, musicians, actors, or writers. Even though it does blunt my creativity somewhat, it has been better for me to be on medication and be able to lead a normal life. Calvin and I were still trying to make a go of things in the wake of my diagnosis. What complicated things was my living with Calvin and his mom in her house. His mother and I started butting heads over stupid things like housework, which I did at odd hours. She grew tired of my strange behavior and threw my clothes down the stairs, probably in frustration and as a signal for me to leave.

Unfortunately, Calvin and I became pregnant a second time a year from the first pregnancy. At this point, I wanted to get married and keep the baby. This time, Calvin wanted me to get an abortion. He said this was because of my medication. He was afraid of birth defects or other possible side effects that could happen to the child. Neither of us researched* this, though. Even though I tried my best to get him to change his mind, he would not budge. My depression was a contributing factor that made it hard for me to muster the energy to fight for the baby. So, sadly, there was a second trip to the clinic, but this time, my dad drove me there and dropped me off. He told Mom it was the worst thing he ever had to do.

Dad apparently drove around until he had to pick me up again. My memory of that day is mostly non-existent. However, this time, I cried afterwards. One of the nurses asked me in a mean tone of voice, "What are you crying about?" I was unable to answer her question and instead turned my face away in shame. It felt like the lowest point in my life. Things could not possibly get any worse, or so I thought. It felt like I was unworthy of God's love, and there was the embarrassment that my family and some friends knew what had happened.

My relationship with Calvin ultimately broke up for good after that. There was no turning back, even after we had dated off and on for nearly five years. Although we had broken up a few times before, this time it was truly and irrevocably over. I ended up moving back home but do not remember where that fell in the sequence of events. At first, the split was fine with me because seeing him only reminded me of all the bad things that had happened and how we had hurt each other. Much later, as I reminisced about the good times we had had, there were thoughts of getting back together while carefully avoiding the thoughts of the pregnancies and abortions.

My attempts to reconnect with Calvin were met with a semi-polite rebuff. When we did not get back together as I had hoped, my emotions sunk lower into depression. At that time, I attributed it to the break-up, much later, I made the connection between the depression and the abortions. After I had moved back home, my bi-polar symptoms were on the depression side. My sister remembered an incident when I was taking a bath. I told her that I had cancer when she came into the bathroom. Another time, I had been in a large shopping mall and somehow got locked in when they closed. There was also a circumstance that involved a shopping spree at the gift shop in the lobby of the hotel where I worked. My mom made me return most of what I had bought because it was frivolous and an unnecessary expense. These incidents showed some classic bi-polar symptoms, which preceded the depression that worsened over time.

Chapter Ten

GETTING FIRED

When the depression first began, it felt manageable. As time progressed, it settled on me like a dark blanket of despair from which there was no escape, nor any possible chance to overcome it. In a way, I allowed myself to slide into the murky pit of my depression. After all, it felt like it was exactly what I deserved. It became hard to get out of bed and face the empty days ahead of me. I no longer cared about my appearance, minimally taking care of my hair. I stopped showering regularly, and putting on make-up seemed pointless; it took too much effort anyway. In any case, the depression made me tired all the time. At my workplace, my boss tried to be patient with me. Since I worked at the front desk of a nice hotel, my appearance was somewhat important. My supervisor was very understanding, but inevitably, she had to let me go. Before I left on my last shift, she said that if I ever felt like I could handle it again, I was welcome to come back. She was such a kind friend in addition to being my supervisor. It felt like she did not really want to fire me, but she had no choice given the circumstances. My normal shift was from three to eleven pm, which worked for me since it did not require getting up early. I have never been a morning person, but unfortunately for me, working second shift meant not being able to hang out with my friends very often. My social life was affected, so that avenue of moral support was not readily available to me. After leaving the hotel that night, everything seemed to be crashing in on me. Problems with my car, the break-up, and my recent job loss added to the heavy load I could not carry anymore. At the age of twenty-two, I felt ready to give up on my life.

*Later in life I researched the effects of medication on having a child and found out there was only one possible issue for an unborn child. It was an anomaly of the heart (possible hole in the heart), which did not happen to my two children, who were born healthy and well.

Chapter Eleven

AFTERMATH OF GETTING FIRED

Thoughts of ways to commit suicide* started to run through my mind. Driving home on a major highway, the first thought was to crash my car into a bridge at a high rate of speed. I had gotten my car up to 100 mph when it started to shake, and it scared me. The thought of what would happen to me if I did not die made me slow down to a more reasonable speed.

On my arrival home, I made a search of the kitchen shelves above the basement for something else to kill myself. Rat poison was on one shelf, but that idea did not appeal to me. My next plan was to cut my own wrists, but I was afraid of the pain. A few bottles of pills sat on the kitchen windowsill; this seemed like a better plan to me. Figuring if I took enough it would do the trick, after swallowing quite a few, I laid on my bed and prepared to die.

However, I did not sleep or die that night. The next day, my mom was making dinner and asked me to get some potatoes, which she kept on the landing of the basement steps. There were still some residual effects from the pills, which nearly caused me to lose my balance and fall. My mom asked me if I was okay, and at first, I told her I was fine. She persisted with more questions, which made me confess everything, including taking the pills. The story of losing my job came out, and I explained how it was the last straw after the break-up with Calvin and problems with my car. It felt like it was the final straw that broke me because I seemed to be dealing with too many problems in my life that threatened to overwhelm me.

Although she was shaken by the news, no action was taken to help me until another incident occurred. Somehow the idea that I had developed cancer in my body continued to torment my mind. These thoughts were telling me to get it out. The way I attempted to accomplish this was jumping up and down, which caused me to urinate on the floor. In my mind, it was the cancer coming out. My mother called the family doctor after this happened. He told her I had lost control and my parents needed to take me to a hospital. Being over the age of twenty-one, it must have been necessary to sign myself in, and yet I have no memory of that.

*Suicide prevention hotline 1-800-273-8255
*Crisis text line-use if you see signs of emotional suffering 1.) Hopelessness 2.) Personality changes 3.) Poor self-care 4.) Withdrawal 5.) Agitation (text SIGNS to 741741)
*Veteran's Crisis Line 1-800-273-8255, press 1
*Crisis Intervention (In PA) 717-394-2631

I wrote "Why is Being Alive an Injustice?" in December of 1981

I seem to feel the pain of living more than other people do,
The sharp edges of reality hurt me, and I wonder why life is so hard at times,

Time ticks inexorably on, it doesn't stop- and the pain gets sharper,

Now I know why some turn to alcohol or drugs…
To soften the edges somewhat, to avoid reality and the pain that it brings,
There just isn't enough time for everything!

Chapter Twelve

First Hospitalization

After my admittance to the hospital, I was taken to a room which already housed another female patient. The doctor introduced us and then showed me and my parents to the day room. He talked to us and asked me a lot of questions. My only recollection of that conversation was when he asked what I thought of my roommate. My thinking was fuzzy and slow due to nearly a week without substantial sleep. My thought process was such that if I did not recall living with someone then I must have really gone off the deep end. I completely misunderstood he meant my hospital roommate, who I had just met. My other answers must have also been somewhat strange because they placed me in the isolation ward instead of the room. This section of the hospital was locked 24/7 with a nurse on duty all the time.

The ward itself was not excessively big. There was a main common room, a bathroom, and four smaller bedrooms without doors. In these smaller rooms, there was hardly any furniture—only a bed, a nightstand, and a lamp. The nurses on duty normally sat at a desk in the main room. The other three patients were all men. There was an older Amish man, a young curly-haired man who seemed close to my age, and a teenage boy with a severe skin condition which grossed me out. This young man insisted on touching my arms all the time. It annoyed me so much, I slapped his arm.

The nurse on duty got angry at me, but I told him; "you tell HIM to stop touching me!" The boy did not bother me after that incident.

In the beginning of my time there, I slept a good bit. It was partly due to my exhaustion and whatever medication the doctor put me on. Once I got caught up on my sleep, I became paranoid about being the only female patient. I began to go to bed holding my hairbrush and planned to use it to defend myself if anyone bothered me. As it turned out, this was not quite the concern that my paranoia led me to believe.

Shortly after that fear was put to rest, delusions started to plague me. I never knew whether they came from my own head or the medications the staff gave me. My first delusion was that I heard an airplane; it had somehow gotten into my head that my grandparents were taking me to Florida. This was not true but may have been the ruse my parents used to get me into the hospital. My grandparents had already gone to Florida for the winter, as they usually did.

Another delusion I had was that I was Stevie Nicks, whose singing voice I admired. My sister Jodi, had shown me an album cover dedicated to someone named Robin. She was probably just calling my attention to it, because she thought it was cool that my name was there.

This may have planted an idea in my head related to the delusion. In addition, I also believed the curly-haired young man in my unit to be Lindsay Buckingham, Stevie's then-boyfriend and bandmate in Fleetwood Mac. All of this may have been a fantasy to escape from the boredom of the ward. The curly-haired patient, who I will call Raymond, seemed perfectly content to play along with this delusion.

The last two delusions were much more bizarre. Somehow, I thought it was possible for me to kill people with my mind. I did not want to do this but felt compelled somehow to do it. This delusion did not last awfully long and was captured in a poem. *(see poem at end of chapter)

The final and most disturbing delusion was the strangest of all. I cannot begin to imagine the origin of this one. I basically stopped eating because my thoughts were telling me that the staff was removing parts of my body while I slept and putting them in my meals during the day. As a result, my weight dropped from 120 pounds to 95-100 pounds. My build was thin to begin with, so I scarcely could afford to lose this weight, ending up being much too thin for my height. My sister said that her and Mom tried to feed me when they visited. Jodi remembers being really worried about my weight loss, and my parents were concerned about this change as well.

The two poems I wrote in this hospital were "I Love All People" and "I Need My Friends"

I love All People *poem related to delusion

I love all people, I have to take a few,
I am afraid of it, of what I have to do,
My heart's too big, loves too many people,
I have to make it smaller, think of myself before other people,
I have to rest, have some time for myself,
Catholic church bells are ringing.

I Need My Friends

I need my friends, I need R------,
I need love, not just physical love,
Forgive me for being so cruel and unfair to you,
I'll be fine if only I'm with you,
You are my hope for tomorrow, my destiny,
Help me adjust to the new you,
I don't know you any longer.
But I do love you with an intensity that frightens me!

Chapter Thirteen

Second Hospital

Mom and Dad had become frustrated with my lack of progress and my extreme weight loss. In speaking with friends of theirs, they found out about a different hospital. It was suggested that this hospital might be a better place to help me. The transfer was arranged, and so I was moved there, but my only thought was to get out of the place. After being in the first hospital for a month, I only wanted to go home. On more than one occasion, I begged my parents to take me home. No doubt, this was not pleasant for them to deal with.

My doctor was an Asian-American gentleman who at least initially seemed very frustrated with me, most likely because I had so much trouble sitting still or even staying in a chair. He first spoke to me in a glass-enclosed room with a lot of plants. I frequently got out of my chair and paced back and forth in a frenetic way. The doctor would ask me to return to my seat and often cleared his throat. It was impossible for me to stay in my chair for any length of time, since there was so much anxiety and nervous energy in my body. He repeatedly asked me to stop getting up, but it was not possible for me to keep my body still.

Eventually, I grew to like my doctor very much, even representing him in a painting as the sun, which I later gave him as a gift. He was the sun because he made me feel more like my old self again and gave me hope for the future. In addition to the counseling sessions with my doctor, there were also art and music therapies. The patients, including myself, could use the gym when it was scheduled.

Although my old delusions were gone, a new one had manifested itself. Whenever I heard water running, it sounded to me like a voice speaking. Fortunately, this was the only delusion I would experience at the second hospital. I started developing crushes on some of the male patients, but nothing further happened from them. However, I did con a sweet guy into giving me his hoodie. Looking back, it still makes me feel bad that I did that to him. It is a common tendency of bi-polar behavior to be manipulative, but that still does not excuse my behavior.

One of my favorite places to hang out at the hospital was the smoker's lounge. Even though I have never smoked, something about the place must have appealed to me. One day, two attractive guys who were visitors came into the lounge. They must have been teasing me because I yelled at them, "Don't mess with me fellas!" The 1981 docudrama *Mommie Dearest* had been released a year or so prior to my hospitalization. In my mind, it was supposed to be a joke as that line was used in the movie. One of the two guys said, "She thinks she's Joan Crawford." Then they both laughed. Their laughter made me angrier than his words had. I knew very well who I was; who was he to make that comment about someone he did not know.

This was not my only difficulty at the second hospital. After I had been there for a month, it bothered me to still be hospitalized and not "better." Also, I had an odd reaction to a medication called Haldol, which was why I called it hound dog! Boredom, though, was probably the hardest thing for me to deal with. It was likely why I wrote so much poetry while I was there. At least it gave me a creative outlet to vent my feelings, which I missed. In school, I had done drawing and painting, as well as other art forms.

There were some good times and memories of my time spent at the second hospital. The patients were permitted to watch the winter Olympics that were broadcast that year. The art and music therapies were enjoyable as well. One of my paintings turned out quite nicely, which pleased me. The painting was an abstract done in layers of watercolor, like something in a dream or under the ocean. I named it *Octopus's Garden*, after The Beatles's song of the same name.

One of the counselors, Ben, was one of my favorite people there. He reminded me of Kenny Rogers in his appearance. He seemed to be in a good mood all the time, always smiling. Being around him helped me feel normal again, which is probably why I liked him so much. My weight was getting back to normal, thanks to the good food at this hospital. The staff had me drink an Ensure every day for good measure. This did not bother me too much as it was usually a chocolate flavor. When my last delusion was gone, I began to feel more like myself every day. My progress was measured by first getting out of the locked ward and being transferred to one with more freedom of movement. As time passed, I was able to enjoy the front porch and later the walking paths on the grounds. I will be always be grateful to my parents who got me into that hospital that gave me the help I needed.

"Peace" & "Linear Notes" were both written in the second hospital.

Peace

Love is all consuming,
No hatred, no wars,

Only peace, love, and tranquility,
All is quiet on the western front,
Love to all,
Only me-Robin

Linear Notes

Calm tranquility of a deep blue sea,
Moods ever shifting, changing sands with the tides,
Moods ever lifting, giving love when I feel like it,
Taking it where I can,

Mate jealous, must find sanity in this realm of despair,
Not feeling so hot,
Sunshine just walked in the door, feels like it anyway,

Haiku good form of self-expression, shows love while taking it,
Too many conch shells around here,
Can anybody help me? No just me, myself, and I (very old for my own health)

Chapter Fourteen

Going Home

At the time of my discharge, my brother Mark came to take me home. It was so good to see him since he had not visited as often as my sister had. My emotions were all over the place, swinging from happiness to anxiety and even fear. It was scary that I did not know what to expect once I got home. Would I be going back to work right away? Could I stay at home and help my family there? What would happen if I had a relapse? My fears were unfounded as my doctor had recommended for me to enter a local day treatment program. The plan was for me to attend the program Monday through Friday for several hours each day. This was an interim form of group counseling which also provided occupational therapy.

It was there that I continued my journey back to wellness and mental stability. The program also provided outings to different places like farmer's markets, parks, or ice cream parlors.

When the time came for me to be discharged from day treatment, I was seen by a therapist at a local clinic. After therapy was deemed no longer necessary, my family doctor took over for my medication checks. These doctor visits involved getting periodic blood tests to ensure my medication was at a therapeutic level in my blood stream. It also gave my doctor the chance to ask me questions about how things were going on the medication, if I needed a prescription refill, or just how my life was going in general. I still see my doctor every six months to a year for these "med" checks, though the doctor just makes sure I have a refill if I need one.

Mom and Dad, Later in Life

Jodi, Mark and I, as Adults

Between the years of 1984 and 1986, my mental health stayed relatively stable. However, there was increased alcohol use, which was likely self-medication on my part. Although I was reliably taking the pills as prescribed, I continued to fight depression as the abortions were never far from my thoughts. My dad and I seemed to be at odds with each other most of the time. He did not like how late I stayed out with my friends. Things came to a head when we had a huge argument. I left the house feeling terribly upset and angry. I raced my car out our road into the fog, going so fast I slid through the stop sign and into a small parking lot. Unperturbed, I continued until I reached the city limits, not particularly caring or paying attention to where I was headed.

Near the city prison there was a red light, and another car zipped into my lane, leaving only inches to spare. There was no attempt to stop on my part, and my car rear ended the other car. The other driver, who was a man, got out and started yelling at me. He was yelling, "You stay there, you stay right there, I'm calling the cops!" It appeared to me that there was no damage to either car, so I chose to leave and drove further into the city. The man followed me, which unnerved me, so I drove to a McDonald's to use their phone.* It was scary that he was still following me, so I called the police and explained what had happened. The officer told me since the accident had happened in the city, it would need to be reported there. After leaving the restaurant, I drove back into the city, but my car ran out of gas**, and I pulled to the side of the road. I did not know what to do next but noticed a house nearby with lights on, so I knocked or rang the bell. Luckily for me, the homeowner let me use his phone. He also gave me a ride to the police station, where I filed the report with a nice female cop. Thank goodness it was a woman because I was pretty rattled by that time. The homeowner drove me back to my car. I believe and hope that I thanked him. He was certainly a good Samaritan in my time of need!

I called my dad for help getting gas, who by this time was very worried and angry with me, rightfully so, I might add. I had really messed up big time this time. I needed to get my act together and get more serious about my future. I felt like I had failed so many times to make my dad proud of me. My next decision was partially prompted by my desire to make my dad proud. I decided that joining the Navy might work since my dad had served in the Navy.

*Note- cell phones did not exist at the time.

**Note- it was common for me to run my car out of gas in those days.

Chapter Fifteen

JOINING THE MILITARY

After my break-up with Calvin and all that followed, this was to be my new beginning. My recruiter asked a lot of questions, so my medical history had to come out. He asked me how badly I wanted to be in the Navy. My response was that I wanted to join the Navy more than anything. The recruiter then told me not to tell the other Navy personnel about my medication and health history. At that time, you could not be on a medication of any kind and be a part of the military.

My plans were all set. All that remained was for me to be sworn in and take the flight to Orlando, Florida, for my basic training. Not long before I left, Calvin called me and then paid me a visit. He was already dating someone else at that time, so when he called and asked to see me, I was surprised. We talked for a bit, and he told me more about his new girlfriend. This was not easy to hear, even though we had been out of our relationship for quite a while. The whole time we talked on my back porch, I felt a bit confused and let down. When he'd said he wanted to see me before I left, I had secretly thought to myself that maybe he wanted to get back together. But this was obviously not the case. When he got ready to leave, my only request was for a final kiss goodbye. Calvin kissed me on the cheek, so I asked him, "Why not on the lips?" He told me his new girlfriend would not like that. There was a sense of finality to our goodbye. It seemed exceedingly clear that I would never see him again. As it turned out, I was right.

My flight to Orlando was basically uneventful, but I was excited to be on my way. When we got into the airport, there was a bus waiting to take the female recruits to the base. After orientation and receiving our uniform items, we were placed in a barracks that housed eighty girls. The barracks was very Spartan in its furnishings, basically just bunkbeds and lockers. The bathroom had communal showers, bathroom stalls, a long mirror, and sinks in a row. There may have been a small common room with chairs, but I really do not remember. This would be home sweet home for the next eight weeks. In the beginning, all of us could not stand each other on sight because we had little in common due to being from many different backgrounds. However, over time, we became friends and gelled as a company. Most of our days were spent marching, drilling, and exercising. Everything we did as a company had consequences. We failed one inspection of our barracks and did not earn a flag for it. Our company commander had our recruit chief petty officer go under all the bunks on her back. She was dusty and dirty after that, and the commander made her get in a clean trash can and say, "Bok, bok, bok, I'm a s--- bird." The military sometimes has a strange way of making a point. In any case, we were one flag short of being an honor company, and we were all pretty bummed out about that.

While in boot camp, my grades were by and large mostly good. My grade point average at the end of boot camp was 3.5, so I was happy about that. The physical demands of the service were extremely difficult at first. Even though I was thin, I was not in good physical condition. Through repeated use of the fitness trail and running laps on the grinder (it was a really big parking lot), my endurance was built up. We also had to pass a swim test in an Olympic-sized swimming pool and drill with fire hoses and go into a smoke house and remove our masks for a period of time. We shot targets with a .22 pistol on a firing range, and those who did well got to shoot a higher caliber gun. We drilled with dummy rifles as well. There was only one time that I can recall that I got into trouble. Although my memory of why I got in trouble is forgotten, I do remember the consequences! I was made to do exercises for at least an hour with a nine-pound dummy rifle. Not fun!

Chapter Sixteen

GRADUATION, APPRENTICESHIP, SECRETS

Further into training, I tried out for and was accepted into the Navy choir. As our unit gradually inched toward graduation, the choir practiced separately for the ceremony from the rest of the company. Toward the end of boot camp, I tried to get someone to cut my hair. There were a few girls within our company who knew how to cut hair, but they were unwilling to help me as I had flirted with their boyfriends. My ill-advised solution was an attempt to cut my own hair, which I had never done before. My company commander flipped out when she saw my terrible haircut and ordered me to get it taken care of on the base. My botched cut was so bad that the stylist had to shave the sides and cut the top extremely short.

Shortly before graduation, I was informed by an officer that I would be unable to perform with the choir due to the appearance of my hair. This made no sense to me since most of it would be covered by my dress cap anyway. In the end, I watched my class graduate while I sat on the bleachers with my family. Even though it was great to see them again, I was still pretty ticked about not being with the choir.

Apprenticeship school began in the week following a weekend of liberty (free time). At this point, I was no longer considered to be a recruit but had become an airman apprentice. In a relatively short period of time after school had started, my bouts with insomnia began. My prescription had run out, and my bi-polar symptoms were beginning to show. The manic or "mood high" phase had begun. I started to show up late or forget assignments altogether. Once I had to get my laundry out of the washer and rush to help screen new recruits after someone else reminded me I was on duty. Around this time, some of my personal articles were stolen, including my military ID. There was no way to be on the base without it. My ID had to be replaced immediately. I had to miss a whole day of classes in order to take care of this. Later, I tried to get class notes from my classmates, but they were "too busy" to help me. These were the same girls whose boyfriends I had flirted with. I fell behind in my classes and seemed to be becoming more forgetful. Eventually a high-ranking female officer confronted me about what was happening.

In a way, it was a relief to be able to finally tell someone the truth. It was then that I came clean about my prescription for bi-polar medication. She immediately informed me that I would be given a medical discharge and that it would be considered honorable. My first response to this was that I wanted to go home right away, but the officer informed me that things did not work that way because there was paperwork to complete. However, instead of going back to my barracks that night as I expected, I was placed in the Naval hospital for the purpose of putting me back on medication and keeping me under observation.

While in the hospital, I recall a conversation with my mom regarding my idea for a commune in Florida. It was to be called "Heaven on Earth." Clearly it was good they were getting me back on medication! While in the hospital, there were some behaviors that the hospital staff asked me to stop doing. Apparently, it was because I was dancing to music in the presence of male patients who were uncomfortable because they found it suggestive. This was my bi-polar condition causing me to do things that were out of character for me. I have no recollection of how long they held me in the hospital. Fortunately for me, it did not seem anywhere near as long as my first hospitalizations had been.

I wrote "Insomnia" many years before the military, but it fits here:

Insomnia

Moon beams alight, softly scattering darkness,
Into patterns of lace, pieces of eight,
Dispersing liquid blackness, into silvery trails,
Quietly the world sleeps.

Chapter Seventeen

BASE HOSPITAL/
HOMEWARD BOUND

Once the medication issue was resolved and the Navy felt I was fit to travel, they gave me the medical discharge and approval to go home. My mom and I spoke on the phone before the trip home. She said I told her I was going to stay in Florida for a weekend of rest and relaxation. (Commonly known in the military as R & R). Mom told me in no uncertain terms that my butt better be on that airplane as planned. She also said she would be picking me up at the airport near our home. Everything went as Mom wanted, and I came home as planned. Unfortunately, not the military career I had envisioned for myself. Even though it was an honorable discharge, once again it felt like I had failed to make my dad proud. I had made a lot of bad choices with men in the past, in the military, and even after my discharge from the hospital.

My feelings of remorse and regret were always close to the surface, even after a great deal of time had passed since the abortions. Although I had had counseling in the hospitals, I am almost certain I did not discuss the abortions with the therapists. I still thought about the children I chose not to have. There was a great fear inside of me that if by some miracle I made it to heaven that then I would have to meet them and explain why I had not wanted them. A Christian friend shared Revelation 21:4 NIV with me, which states, "He will wipe every tear from their eyes and there will be no more death or sorrow or crying or pain, for the old order of things has passed away." She also told me that when I met them, all would be well.

There were many times I asked God for forgiveness, yet I still did not feel forgiven. It never occurred to me that God forgave me the first time I asked Him and meant it. It turned out that the hardest thing to do was to forgive myself, and when I was finally able to accomplish this, I experienced what I felt was an incomplete peace. It would be many years before I would know lasting peace. This peace is the kind only Jesus can give. John 14:27 NIV says, "Peace I leave with you; my peace I give you. I do not give to you as the world gives; do not let your hearts be troubled and do not be afraid."

In the eight years between when my relationship with Calvin ended and the year I met my husband, I was kind of lost. It took a long time for me to find my way back to God. All I ever wanted in my life was to have someone love me. I tried to create relationships through physical intimacy, which only led to empty, meaningless relationships. I continued to lean on alcohol to dull my mental pain and chase away unpleasant memories.

Chapter Eighteen

HUSBAND & CHILDREN I

It was when I met my husband at the age of thirty and we welcomed two children into our family that my healing seemed more complete. It felt like God still loved me and was giving me a second chance. At our rehearsal dinner, I told my father-in-law-to-be that it was as if God had brought John and I together; in other words, we were meant to be. His dad seemed to get a bit emotional after I said that, and he was typically like my dad in that he did not often show his emotions! John and I were starting out in less than perfect circumstances. We had not known each other for a long period of time, and we already had a baby on the way. Neither of my children were planned pregnancies. Our children were born sixteen months apart, which seemed to be the mirror image of my earlier pregnancies. Praise God for His grace and mercy. John and our children have been such a blessing for me. Although we really struggled the first five years, we persevered and made it work. John and I met in July of 1990 and were married by December of the same year.

Our Wedding Day

When our children were born and I held them for the first time, it was impossible to imagine loving anyone more. God loves us to an even greater degree than a mother's love, as pure and limitless as it might seem. Being a mother brought out all the protective instincts I never knew I had. I had never had anyone so dependent on me for all their needs. God is much like a human parent who always wants to protect us, care for us, and have us trust Him completely. As much as I loved my dear daughter (my firstborn), Renee drove me crazy in her first three months of life due to colic, which made her cry for hours. I tried everything possible to help her, but only two things worked—the vacuum cleaner with limited success and car rides. Riding in the car was the only sure-fire way to lull her to sleep. Fortunately, she outgrew the colic and became a much calmer baby. Our son Eric was an easier newborn, which made life with two children a bit easier than I had imagined.

Being silly

Renee, Eric, and Chelsea

I love to sing and often sung hymns and popular songs as lullabies for our little ones. One of my favorites to sing was usually "Golden Slumbers" by The Beatles. It is possibly why Renee became a Beatles fan later in her life. Although I used to read to our children every day, neither of my children are avid readers like me. When our children became toddlers, it was a constant activity to chase them and check on them because they got into everything! My husband John worked two jobs when our kids were young, so he was either sleeping or working most of the time. This left me in charge of the children by myself for a good percentage of the days and nights.

Once both of our children were able to walk, what one of them did not think of, the other one did. They both constantly dragged things out of cupboards, dumped laundry baskets, and generally made messes. On one occasion, my phone conversation went a bit long with my mother-in-law, and they got into the Desiten ointment. It was likely Renee who climbed into the playpen and got it out of the diaper bag. When I went to check on her and Eric, they were covered head to toe in the ointment! It was also on the couch, end table, and rug. Both kids had to be scrubbed in the bathtub. Desiten is not easy to get off! With Renee and Eric being so active and noisy, it became necessary to take them out on many walks to keep the house quiet for my husband John. He generally slept during the day due to his working night shift. Another solution was spending time with my sister and her children since our kids got along and played nicely together. Despite their tendency to get into trouble together and sometimes get on each other's nerves, Renee and Eric were good friends and playmates most of the time. In fact, another mom in a doctor's office once asked me if they always got along so well. This seemed to annoy her, so I told her it was not anything I had done. They were just close together in age and development.

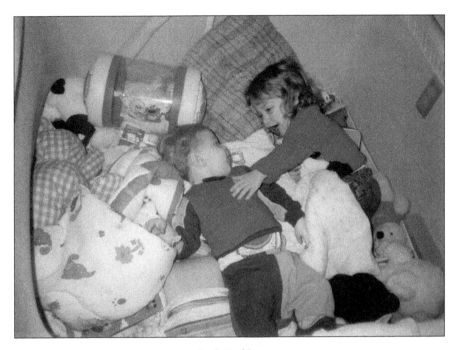

Little Buddies

As Renee and Eric became school aged, things got easier. The biggest difficulty during that time was the daily battle over Eric not doing his homework, which resulted in him losing privileges. Eric also became the "fairness police." He claimed that everything his sister got or had was bigger or better than what he had. At some point, he went through a firebug stage. It became necessary to find better hiding places for matches and lighters so he would not be able to find them. One day, I caught Eric lighting a birthday candle using the gas stove burner. After the candles were hidden too, I invited a firefighter to speak to both of our children about the dangers of fire. Eventually this stage passed, and the concern about a possible house fire was put to rest.

Eric, Chelsea, and Renee as Teenagers

In her early teen years, Renee went through a phase of slamming doors when she was angry, typically at her brother Eric. Even after I had asked her to stop several times, she did not comply until she lost some privileges. The teenage years were comparable to the toddler age in that there was more testing and pushing boundaries. Renee became protective of her room and belongings. She also started to get a bit smart-mouthed. At one point, without thinking about it, I slapped her on her face. Later, I apologized and told her she could not talk to me like that, in such a disrespectful way. The slap surprised me as much as it did her, as I had never done that before or after that incident. Consequently, she never spoke to me in that manner again.

In his teen years, Eric started to isolate himself in his room and seemed depressed. My attempts to speak to him about this got stonewalled. He always told me he was okay, though much later I found some of his writings, which talked about suicide. Eric would not talk to me about anything dealing with his emotions, but it was obvious to me he was going through some tough emotional times. At one point, he ran away from home, and I was terrified. He would not answer when I called his cell phone or return my texts. I reached out to his girlfriend on Facebook, and she got him to meet me at a Dunkin' Donuts, which was where we were able to talk, and he agreed to come home. It was a great relief to me when he outgrew his rebellious ways, but his teenage years were not easy for me.

My children have given me my greatest joys and sometimes my greatest sorrows. Regardless of the difficulties I encountered over the course of parenting them, I am so glad God blessed me with them. Though I did not play as much of a parental role in Chelsea's life, I hope that mine has been a good influence on her. In any case, I love her as much as I do Renee and Eric. John and I have become closer with our children as they became young adults. They have grown to be good people, and we are so proud of them. The hardest part of parenting young adults is learning to let them go and make their own mistakes. As much as I would like to protect them, all I can do at this point is give my best advice and hope they listen. I do pray for them a lot!

Our relationship with God is much like this. He does not stop us from making mistakes but does help us through the consequences of our decisions. We need to heed His wise counsel and pray about any questions or confusion we may have. We can put all our trust in God. He is trustworthy and keeps His promises in His perfect timing. Our way of understanding time is far different from God's way. To Him, a day can be the same as a thousand years. Isaiah 55:8 NIV reads, "'For my thoughts are not your thoughts, neither are your ways my ways, declares the Lord'

Chapter Nineteen

HUSBAND & CHILDREN II

At the time of this writing, John and I have been married for nearly thirty years. It has not been easy, and we have had to work at it every day to keep our relationship on track. During our first five years, I nearly threw in the towel because of how much we struggled. This was mostly due to poor communication skills on both of our parts. Instead of giving up, though, we chose to talk things out and make it work.

As a couple, we have dealt with many trials over the years. We had to file bankruptcy after we had lived in our first home for only a few years due to an adjustable-rate loan. When we moved to our next house, which we rented, we had two floods that filled our basement with water and left us with a few inches on the first floor both times. John worked night shift the whole time our kids were growing up, and while this was difficult for me, it meant we did not need child-care in their preschool years. Not long after we bought our current home, John lost a significant percentage of his salary due to corporate greed.

View from Carport

Foot Bridge Covered by Water

We were left trying to figure out how we would be able to pay our mortgage with a smaller paycheck. Refinancing was the only way we were able to keep our home. The most difficult of all was losing both of our dads and my grandparents in just one year.

Yes, our relationship has seen its share of adversity, but we got through it all together. God has been so good to us, and John and I have become each other's best friends. Even with all the trials we have experienced, the good has always outweighed the bad. John and I put our trust in God, and we know He holds our future in His hands, whatever that might be.

"A Prayer for Us" and "You Make Me Happy, When."

A Prayer for Us

Oh Lord give us strength to meet the challenges of our new life together,
Give us the courage to deal with life's adversities when they come our way,
Help us to be patient with each other, that we may understand each other's needs and concerns from day to day,
Help our love to endure despite many pressures, and worries of everyday life,
Give us guidance to be good examples and teachers for our children,
Lord we know that with your loving hand, our marriage will be a happy and successful one,
Rough times not- withstanding, we ask that you watch over us, guide us, and give us strength,
That we might grow in love.

You Make Me Happy When – see below

You make me happy when you smile or we share a laugh,
You make me happy when you don't get mad at my latest gaffe,
You make me happy when you appreciate something I've done,
You make me happy when you make me feel like I'm your special #1,
You make me happy when you have a good time with our kids,
You make me happy when you surprise me with something you did,
But most of all, you've made me feel happy and well-loved,
And for that, and more, I thank the good Lord above!

Chapter Twenty

STRUGGLES WITH FAITH

Even though I finally had everything I wanted in life—a husband, children, and a home—there was a feeling of being incomplete inside me. Something was missing, and I did not know what it was. Eventually, I realized it was my relationship with God. It felt like I was putting on a show of faith, an imitation of the real thing. I felt like I was a "counterfeit Christian," having an appearance of being a person of faith without the deep roots. My journey back to God and faith began after our children were born. When they got old enough to walk, I started taking them to church with me. My intention was to give them a foundation of faith as I had had. They attended church with me at least until they were in early high school.

My own faith was tested in August of 2007. I got a phone call around 2:00 am. It was my mom telling me my dad had had a stroke. Of course, I could not sleep after that call, so I told John I was going to the emergency room to be with my mom. Initially, we did not know much about Dad's condition other than that he had suffered a severe stroke. The two things that helped me get through the aftermath of the stroke was writing and talking to God. Many nights, I cried, prayed, and read my Bible. The writing helped me process what had happened to my dad and how my family dealt with it.

In the beginning of his hospitalization, Dad was in the trauma unit in an unconscious state for a month. When he came out of the coma, he was unable to talk, eat, or even move much, and we did not know what to expect.

Dad was mostly confined to bed for the last four and a half years of his life. I struggled to understand why God would allow him to live like that for so long. There were no answers to my questioning thoughts. Sometimes we do not ever learn what purpose an experience like that serves. At that time, my doubts seemed bigger than my faith, but I continued to seek answers by going to church, praying, and reading my Bible. This poem was written sometime after my dad's stoke:

A Prayer

I don't know what to think,
And I don't know what to feel,

Somehow reality seems terribly surreal,

It hurts to think this present
Might be all we could expect, so…

I don't want to think
And I don't want to feel,

This fear in my heart,
I want to reject,

Lord take it away,

Ease my mind and
Quiet my troubled thoughts,

Give me strength to meet
The challenges of the coming days,

And regardless of my circumstances,
I will always pray.

On the morning before my dad's death, I was getting ready for work as I usually did. Out of nowhere, a part of a hymn came to my head: "On Christ the solid rock I stand, all other ground is sinking sand, all other ground is sinking sand."* I dismissed it as a random thought and went to work. In the middle of my workday, my husband called with the news that my dad's condition was worsening. As I left work and got closer to the retirement home, a fragment of Scripture popped into my head. "God perfects us in our weakness." ** That kind of blew my mind. It also made me cry a little, and I said a slightly stunned thank you to God. This was something that had never happened to me before. I was so thankful that God made Himself known to me in a more tangible way that day. God is always there when we need Him, whether we realize it or not. My dad passed away the next day. That evening, my mom, John, Renee, and I went to say goodbye to him at the nursing home. It was so strange seeing him after he was gone, and there were no tears because I had cried so many tears after the stroke had happened. We had mourned for him from the time he had had the stroke. I clung to God and John during this prolonged grieving period, and I continued to read my Bible and pray. To this day, I still have many unanswered questions. Maybe someday I will have answers, but even if those answers do not come, my trust in God will never be shaken.

- "My Hope Is Built" hymn- words by Edward Mote, 1834 and music by William B. Bradbury, 1863

**2 Corinthians 12:9 (NLT)-

"Each time he said, 'My grace is all you need, My power works best in weakness.' So now I am glad to boast about my weaknesses, so that the power of Christ can work through me."

This letter was written in November 2018 – a memorial to my dad, and a symbol of my changed relationship with him.

Dear Dad,

You are in my thoughts today because tomorrow is Veteran's Day. I think of you many times, but Veteran's Day made me think of you now. I don't have any more unforgiveness toward you for the past for all the times we were at odds with each other. The more I write my story, the more I realize you loved us in the best way you knew how. In our limited human way, nobody loves perfectly; only Jesus did. I started to learn to love you when we had our big argument. It touched me that you cried because of the words I spoke from my heart. I do love you, Dad, and I'm glad for the good years we had together. I miss you, as I'm sure your grandchildren do, especially Renee. You and she had a special bond. It made me happy to see how good you were with your grandchildren; you loved them well. It also made me happy when you were able to give (us kids) hugs and kisses.

My heart treasured the words you spoke to me when you said I was a good mom. That meant more to me than you will ever know. I hope that I am indeed a good mom; in any case, I am doing the best I can. I pray that I'm being a good example for them. I learned a lot from you—the value of hard work, doing a job well, taking care of your belongings, keeping things tidy, and a love of animals. As I get older, I see more of your family traits in my appearance. Anyhow, I do love you, Dad, and miss you.

Love, Robin

Renee Coloring with Pop-pop

Chapter Twenty-one

CREATION FESTIVAL/
TRULY SAVED

Two years after Dad's death, God stepped into my life in the form of my friend Penny. We had met in the lunchroom of our workplace. We talked about many things including God and faith. After many shared lunchtime conversations, we decided to camp together at Creation Festival, which is held at the end of June in Mount Union, Pennsylvania.

Penny and I planned our food and camping gear for our trip, and we were on our way! It took a little over two hours to get there and then set everything up. It was so amazing to be there with so many people of faith enjoying the music and speakers together. For a quite a few years, I had attended a church and considered myself to be a Christian. But I had never given Jesus my whole heart; everything inside of me, the good, the bad, and even the ugly. Everything at Creation radiated God's love from the music to the seminars. God clearly communicated with those who came to listen. Penny and I attended the main stage for as many concerts and speakers as we could. Every evening, the speaker offered interested attendees the opportunity to join in reciting the sinner's prayer of salvation. *See footnote at end of chapter.

Penny and I at Creation 2014

Later in the weekend, fate or God (or probably both!) stepped in again. My friend and I had gotten separated, and it would not be easy to find her in such large crowd. In order to see my cell phone better to text her, I went into a tent, which turned out to be the prayer tent. One of the volunteers inside asked if I wanted prayer for anything while I was there. I suggested praying for people in my family who needed to come to Christ. Then the volunteer asked if I had any other prayer requests to share, and initially, nothing came to mind. She asked me if I had ever said the sinner's prayer. I said that during the past few days, I had said it many times, though I did not believe it was necessary for me personally. As we talked more at length and I shared about my past, I then realized that, yes, I did need to say that prayer for myself!

The volunteers were so easy to talk to that I was able to confess everything heavy on my heart. These kind ladies then asked me to join them in the sinner's prayer again. When we finished the prayer, all the pain and weight from the past were gone! I finally felt free! Free of all the sins from my past, including the abortions. These kind ladies asked if I wanted to be baptized in the pond the next day, and my new conversion experience prompted me to sign up on the spot.

So many people loved and encouraged me to take that next step—my friend Penny, of course, but also my new friends I had met at Creation, Dan and his daughter Mary and Sara. Sara told me God had been pursuing me my whole life, and she was right. I was so excited by these events that I stayed up late talking with everyone. When I did get into bed, it was hard to get to sleep with so many thoughts going through my head.

On Saturday, all the people getting baptized gathered in the prayer tent, and a volunteer explained the building blocks of faith. When we went to the pond to be baptized, things got a bit confusing. There were so many people around the pond watching that it was hard to tell who was being baptized. It took me a few minutes to realize that unless I went around the people blocking the water, I would not get baptized. As I started to wade into the pond, I asked a woman nearby to take a picture for me. She agreed, so I handed her my disposable camera. She took both a before and an after picture, and I hugged her and thanked her afterwards. The crowd was so big that I did not see my friends until the baptisms were over. Everyone gave me hugs, even though I was soaking wet! I had met so many wonderful people who had beautiful hearts for God at Creation. My belief is that God brought Penny into my life and into my workplace so we could go to Creation together. I will always be thankful that Penny camped there with me so I could be truly saved. My heart and mind are FINALLY at peace with the past!

Note: There are many different versions of this prayer, and all of them help lead people to salvation.

This one is from the Billy Graham Evangelistic Association.

- Dear God, I know I'm a sinner, and I ask for Your forgiveness. I believe Jesus Christ is Your Son. I believe He died for my sin and that You raised Him to life. I want to trust Him as my Savior and follow Him as Lord from this day forward. Guide my life and help me do Your will. I pray this in the name of Jesus. Amen.

If you have prayed this prayer (or one similar), welcome to the family of God! Your next step is to seek a loving, Bible-believing church to continue to grow in your new-found faith. It helps to be part of a community of believers, even more so to be a member of a small group where believers can learn, grow, and be accountable to each other. I cannot emphasize that enough—small groups are the life blood of the church. They are the best way to grow your faith by praying and studying God's Word together!

I wrote "Faith Comes Hard" in more recent years:

Faith… comes hard to a sinner like me,
So often seeming blind, refusing to see,
Truth…shining like a beacon before my face,
My sin-filled life saved by God's abundant grace,
Learning to be still and trust,
Trying hard to obey,

These wonderful words, always encouraging, hold true yet today,
Give me hope for tomorrow…
God's love and grace will ease all my sorrows.

Chapter Twenty-two

GROWING IN FAITH

I have come to be secure in the knowledge that Jesus is my Savior, and I am free at last in Him. It is such a wonderful thing to be forgiven by God! God offers this forgiveness to all who confess their sins and believe Jesus Christ died for their sins, no matter how terrible they might be. If we repent and are sorry for what we have done, God forgives. We are still judged at the end of our lives, but we are found not guilty of our sins by the blood of Christ. *John 3:16 says, "For God so loved the world that he gave his only Son, that whoever believes in him will not perish but have eternal life" (NIV).

For so many years, I was burdened by the sins of my past. I was held in bondage until I trusted Jesus to set me free of the heavy load I was carrying. Thank goodness it got left behind at Creation 2014! My faith has grown since that time, and my life has been so much better in every way. I am thankful to be able to see God through new eyes. Other than my relationship with God, my family and friends are my greatest treasures. Without Jesus, I would still be living in the spiritual darkness of my old life. My renewed life has blessed me with a lightness of spirit and a feeling of well-being and freedom that I never felt before. As well as developing the ability to pray meaningfully, I have learned to trust God more each day. I now have the desire to talk about my faith with others and share what God has done in my life.

We as people desperately need Jesus in our lives. We live in a dark and sin-filled world. Christians can make a difference by allowing Christ's light to shine in the darkness through them. Acts of mercy, kindness, and love show the world what belonging to Christ is all about. It takes commitment and dedication to follow the way of Christ. As Christians, we need to be vigilant to protect ourselves from allowing other idols to take the place of God. Careers, hobbies, sports, working out, and the media are common substitutions for that spot in our lives. These things in and of themselves are not sinful, but when they take priority over God, they are becoming idols. Even the people we love can become an idol if we place them above God in importance. Exodus 20:3 says, "You shall have no other Gods before me." NIV

Living out my faith day to day has its share of ups and downs. Reading and studying God's Word helps keep me on track. Having fellowship with other Christians also helps make the journey easier. Matthew 18:20 says, "Whenever two or three are gathered in my name, there am I with them." NIV Praying to God for what you need and thanking Him for what you have is a good faith-building practice.

An attitude of gratitude is important to cultivate as a Christian. When we get into the habit of being thankful for our blessings, the things we lack seem less important. Writing this testimony seemed next to impossible when I first started putting it on paper. It was overwhelming, to say the least! However, through reading Christian literature and scriptures, God made it seem possible. God helped me make my dream of writing a book a reality. Matthew 19:26 (NIV) reads, Jesus looked at them and said, "With man this is impossible, but with God all things are possible." What is your dream? What could God be calling you to do for His glory? All of us are gifted with a talent that we can use to glorify God. It could be anything! If you go to God in prayer and keep yourself open to His plan for you, the answer might surprise you!

You may wonder if my life is perfect since becoming a believer. Absolutely not! Do I still have doubts and fears? Yes, of course I do! My goal each day is to live faithfully and trust God. God does not promise us a trouble-free life, but He does promise in Matthew 28:20 b, "And be sure of this, I am with you always, even to the end of the age." NLT

The past is over; don't let it define you! The future is not yet here; don't allow worries about it to steal your joy! The present is here and now, trust God, and live each day as it comes to you. Every day we get to choose whether we will be thankful for the gift of time God has given us or waste it in useless worry and stress. Matthew 6:27 says, "Can all your worries add a single moment to your life?" Verse 33 says, "Seek the kingdom of God above all else and live righteously and He will give you everything you need." NLT

God has fundamentally changed how I handle relationships with other people. I have learned to forgive those who I perceive to have wronged me (regardless of the offense). In addition, God has shown me how to examine my own behavior, and I have also learned to ask forgiveness from both God and people for things I have done to hurt or offend them. In the past, I led a mostly un-examined and selfish life.

God has opened my heart and mind to take the focus away from myself, and be willing to serve Him and His people.

"My Broken and Contrite Heart" was written in November of 2018

My broken and contrite heart,
My broken and contrite heart,

Is all I have to give him,

Is all I have to give him,

My wounded soul,

My wounded soul…belongs to Him alone,

In Him is the way, in him is the truth, and in Him is the life,

I know that full well,

He is my healer, my redeemer, my all in all,

Nothing can separate me from the love of God,

Nothing can keep me from my Lord, my rock, my Savior.

Chapter Twenty-three

QUESTIONS AND ANSWERS

Q.) Did I have negative thoughts associated with God? A.) Most definitely, largely due to the magnitude of my past sins. Also, I characterized God as being like my earthly father: disapproving, unforgiving, and hard to please (at least until my relationship with my dad improved.)

Q.) Did thoughts of God bring me shame? A.) There is no doubt that shame was the emotion I most associated with God and my relationship with Him in my younger years. I had committed some terrible sins and did not feel God could ever forgive me for them.

Q.) What questions was I asking of myself in my poetry? A.) A great deal of my poetry dealt with my unsuccessful search for love. It communicated my longing to love and be loved. If I had understood the true nature of God, I would not have needed to look for love outside of a relationship with Him. Much of my poetry was an attempt to express raw emotions inside of me, the deep pain and sense of loss, as well as the negative feelings of self-worth related to the abortions.

Q.) Why didn't I share with my family or friends? A.) I was living in my own personal world of pain, depression, and torment. I didn't understand that the abortions had caused the feelings and not the external factors I blamed for them. It was my intent to hide the guilt and shame from everyone including my family.

Q.) Why didn't I get closure/work through things? A.) The depression and subsequent breakdown prevented me from getting closure. The guilt and pain were a constant loop running in my mind. After my recovery from the depression, it took me a long time to recognize why I didn't feel forgiven.

Q.) What was the first time I felt compelled to talk to those around me? A.) My mother was the first person I was truthful with about what was going on with me. It took me years to get at the root cause of the depression, breakdown, and suicide attempt. My poem "A Mother's Heart" was an "aha" moment that gave me insight into the real cause of what I went through.

Q.) What made me thankful to God? A.) Although in the beginning I felt deserted by God, I never stopped crying out to Him in prayer and poetry. With the distance I now have from that time, it has become clear to me that God was always there! My life has changed so drastically from that time that it's almost like a bad dream. God has been so good to me in so many ways. My husband and I have been married for nearly thirty years. We have three beautiful children between us (John has a daughter from his previous marriage.) For most of my life, I have been blessed with the gift of writing, which has helped me through some dark days. He has given me this testimony to share. God has seen me through so many things in my life and has brought me out of the darkness into the light!

Q.) How has God spoken to me through this experience? A.) God has shown me that I can be a blessing to others dealing with experiences like mine: people who have or have had mental health issues as I did and women who have considered or have had an abortion. Unfortunately, mental health disorders still have a stigma attached to them without reason. The brain is a part of the body, the same as any other. Mental health is just as, if not more, important than physical health. As for abortion, it has become a hot button topic that politicians like to use in campaigns like a weapon. I got a second chance to be a mother, and the privilege of raising our children has been a blessing. I am now pro-life and believe abortion is wrong; however, I believe I have been called to minister to both women who have had abortions as well as those who are considering it. My personal experience showed me that mental breakdowns sometimes follow this type of surgery. When I was given a second chance to have children, my choice was to give birth to them. Because of my past choices, I have no right to judge anyone, and as a Christian, well, after all, we are to judge not lest we be judged by the same measure.

A final note: My hope is that God will use this story to bless, encourage, and minister to those who feel like I used to feel, a counterfeit Christian. May God bless you and keep you. He loves you for exactly who He created you to be. Romans 12:4 & 5 NLT says, "Just as our bodies have many parts and each part has a special function, so it is with Christ's body. We are many parts of one body, and we all belong to each other. In his grace God has given us different gifts for doing certain things well."

In this book, I have attempted to strike a balance between a fair representation of my family while being truthful about myself and my past. However, in all honesty I gave my dad plenty of reasons to be angry or disappointed in me. The lines between what behavior I was responsible for and what was likely caused by my bi-polar are still hard for me to distinguish from each other. My breakdown and hospitalization were no doubt as hard, if not worse, for my parents than they were for me. I thank God that my mom and dad saw me through that time and that I have become a stronger person and Christian because of my trials. God refines us in the fiery trials we go through. Our faith becomes stronger and more solid when we suffer trials because God helps us to endure them and persevere.

> James 1:2-4 NIV reads, "Consider it pure joy, my brothers and sisters, whenever you face trials of many kinds, because you know that the testing of your faith produces perseverance. Let perseverance finish its work so that you may be mature and complete, not lacking anything."

Amen-The End!

CPSIA information can be obtained
at www.ICGtesting.com
Printed in the USA
BVHW040248260322
632265BV00008B/276